I want to be a
BALLET DANCER

PowerKiDS press

New York

Mary R. Dunn

Dedicated to Brianna

Published in 2009 by The Rosen Publishing Group, Inc.
29 East 21st Street, New York, NY 10010

First Edition

Editor: Amelie von Zumbusch
Book Design: Ginny Chu
Layout Design: Julio Gil
Photo Researcher: Jessica Gerweck

Photo Credits: Cover, p. 8 Shutterstock.com; pp. 4, 6, 10, 14, 20 © AFP/Getty Images; p. 12 © Getty Images; p. 16 © Time & Life Pictures/Getty Images; p. 18 © Associated Press.

Library of Congress Cataloging-in-Publication Data

Dunn, Mary R.
   I want to be a ballet dancer / Mary R. Dunn.
      p. cm. — (Dream jobs)
   Includes index.
   ISBN 978-1-4042-4469-6 (library binding)
   1. Ballet—Juvenile literature. 2. Ballet dancing—Juvenile literature. 3. Ballet dancers—Juvenile literature.
I. Title.
   GV1787.5.D86 2009
   792.8–dc22
                                    2007049624

Manufactured in the United States of America

Contents

The ballet *Swan Lake* tells the sad story of a woman who was turned into a swan and a prince who falls in love with her.

Spinning and Jumping!

Do you like music and dancing? If so, you might like to learn ballet. Ballet is a beautiful, **graceful** form of dance. Ballet dancers learn exact ways to move their bodies. They use this knowledge to spin, turn, and jump in shows called ballets. Many ballets tell a story. Some ballets, such as *Cinderella* and *Sleeping Beauty*, take their stories from well-known fairy tales.

Ballet dancers spend years learning about and practicing ballet. Highly skilled dancers, like Maria Tallchief and Rudolf Nureyev, have become well known and made ballet a great art form.

These ballerinas, or female ballet dancers, are dancing *en pointe* in the ballet *Giselle*. Dancing *en pointe* takes lots of skill and practice.

The Story of Ballet

The story of ballet began long ago. In the 1600s, King Louis XIV of France gave big parties at his palace. At these parties, people watched dancers **perform**. Louis loved dance. He started a school called the Royal Academy of Dance. At the school, dancers were taught five special positions in which to hold their feet and hands. All modern ballet is based on these positions.

Today, dancers still learn the same five positions. They learn dance movements that build on these basic positions, too. For example, skilled female ballet dancers learn to dance *en pointe*, or on their toes.

This young ballet dancer is practicing at a barre. Barres often have one bar for dancers to rest their hands on and another for their feet.

Ready? Plié!

Boys and girls who want to learn ballet take classes at a dance school. Finding a good school and teacher is important. The School of American Ballet and the Joffrey Ballet School are two of the most famous schools in the United States.

In most ballet classes, dancers begin by standing tall and practicing at the **barre**. The dancers do exercises, like **pliés**. Later, the dancers move to the center of the room to do exercises to learn **balance**. Ballet class ends with a *révérence*, or thank-you bow to the teacher.

These dancers are members of the Smuin Ballet, a ballet company from San Francisco, California.

Finding a Ballet Family

Young dancers who want to be **professionals** must become part of a company. The San Francisco Ballet and the American Ballet Theatre are two important American dance companies.

To **join** a company, a dancer must audition. An audition is a test of dancing skills. The director of the company watches the dancers perform and chooses only the best for the company. The dancers who make it through auditions are called apprentices, or beginners. The most skilled members of companies are the principal dancers. They have the lead parts in a company's ballet performances.

Dancers often wear tights and a tight-fitting piece of clothing called a leotard to practice ballet.

Practicing and Preparing

The members of a company work together to get ready for a performance. Dancers practice moving in time to the music. They learn all the movements for their dances. Dancers learn when to pirouette, or spin, and when to do a *grand jeté*, or long jump. Dancers in ballets that use mime, or noiseless acting, learn mime movements, too. Dancers rehearse, or practice, every day.

During breaks from practicing, dancers get fitted for **costumes**. Hats, wigs, **tutus**, shirts, and tights make dancers look like the roles, or parts, they are dancing.

In *The Nutcracker*, a girl travels to a land of sweets, where she sees dances honoring treats from around the world.

14

Opening Night

Opening night is the first time that dancers perform a ballet for an **audience**. The dancers arrive at the **theater** early. They warm up by practicing at the barre. They put on their costumes and makeup and fix their hair.

After the lights dim and the **orchestra** starts playing, the show begins! The dancers bring music and stories to life. Some ballets, like *The Nutcracker*, are happy stories. Many, like *Swan Lake* and *Giselle*, end sadly. At the end of the ballet, the dancers bow. The audience claps and shouts, "Bravo!"

Julie Kent is one of the American Ballet Theatre's principal dancers. She has also appeared in the movie *Center Stage*.

Famous Ballet Dancers

Skilled ballet dancers who take part in many performances can become famous. One famous American ballet dancer is Julie Kent. She is a member of the American Ballet Theatre and has danced many roles. In 2000, Kent became the first American to win the Prix Benoit de la Danse, an important ballet **prize**.

Mikhail Baryshnikov is one of the world's most famous ballet dancers. He started taking lessons in Riga, Latvia, when he was 12. He performed in Russia but later came to America. After he grew too old to dance professionally, Baryshnikov became a **choreographer**.

Retired dancer Arthur Mitchell became a well-liked teacher. He formed a ballet company called the Dance Theatre of Harlem.

18

Ballet Teachers

Ballet requires lots of strength. It is hard on a dancer's body. Most dancers retire, or stop performing, by the time they are in their 40s. Dancers often become teachers when their performance days are over. Retired dancers often make good teachers.

Ballet teachers watch students carefully during class. Teachers call out directions to dancers as they exercise at the barre. Sometimes a teacher taps a dancer's foot or arm to correct a wrong position. Teachers also tell dancers when they have done well. Most of all, good teachers make dancing fun!

The ballet *Serenade* was choreographed by George Balanchine. Balanchine is most likely ballet's best-known choreographer.

Choreographers

While some retired ballet dancers teach, others become choreographers. Choreographers decide the positions and movements dancers will use in a performance. Choreographers generally know how to dance, so they often show dancers the movements they want to see performed. Sometimes, choreographers ask dancers to move freely to music. Choreographers make notes of the movements they see and choose some to use in a dance.

Choreographers do not work alone. They plan with other people, like costume makers and artists, so that scenes and ballet movements fit together well.

Becoming a Ballet Dancer

If you want to become a ballet dancer, you must prepare your body for hard work. Dancers have to exercise and eat the right foods. Most importantly, dancers need to take classes and practice ballet positions, steps, and movements.

Being a ballet dancer is hard, but it can be wonderful, too. When the dancers in a ballet company work well together, they have lots of fun practicing and performing. They give joy to audiences, too, by taking them into the wonderful world of stories, music, and dance.

Glossary

audience (AH-dee-ints) A group of people who watch or listen to something.

balance (BAL-ens) Staying steady.

barre (BAHR) A bar or set of bars that is used in ballet classes.

choreographer (kor-ee-AH-gruh-fer) A person who creates dances.

costumes (kos-TOOMZ) Clothes that make a person look like someone or something else.

graceful (GRAYS-ful) Smooth and beautiful.

join (JOYN) To come together or take part in.

orchestra (OR-kes-truh) A group of people who play music together.

perform (per-FORM) To do something for other people to watch.

pliés (plee-AYZ) Ballet movements in which the knees are bent and the back is held straight.

prize (PRYZ) A thing that can be won.

professionals (pruh-FESH-nulz) People who are paid for what they do.

theater (THEE-uh-tur) A building where a performance is held.

tutus (TOO-tooz) Short skirts worn in ballet performances.

Index

A
audience(s), 15, 22

B
balance, 9
barre, 9, 15, 19

C
choreographer(s),
17, 21
Cinderella, 5

costumes, 13, 15

F
fairy tales, 5

M
music, 5, 13, 15,
21–22

O
orchestra, 15

P
professionals, 11

S
show(s), 5, 15
Sleeping Beauty, 5
story, 5, 7, 15, 22

T
theater, 15
tutus, 13

Web Sites

Due to the changing nature of Internet links, PowerKids Press has developed an online list of Web sites related to the subject of this book. This site is updated regularly. Please use this link to access the list:
www.powerkidslinks.com/djobs/ballet/